FAITH VS FAITHFULNESS

A PRIMER ON REST

JON MOFFITT   JUSTIN PERDUE
JIMMY BUEHLER

Copyright © 2019 by Theocast, Inc.

Scripture quotations are from the Holy Bible, English Standard Version, copyright © 2001 by Crossway Bibles, a publishing ministry of Good News Publishers. Used by permission. All rights reserved. All rights reserved. No part of this book may be reproduced, stored in a retrieval system, or transmitted in any form or by any means—electronic, mechanical, photocopy, recording, or otherwise—except for brief quotations for the purpose of review or comment, without the prior permission of the publisher, Theocast, Inc.

Theocast, Inc. www.theocast.org

This book is dedicated to the many who have supported our ministry, enabling us to advance the gospel of Jesus Christ. May you find rest in Him.

CONTENTS

Introduction	vii
What Is Pietism?	1
What Is Confessionalism?	4
How Do I Know If I'm in a Pietistic Context?	6
How Confessionalism Leads to Rest	12
New Creatures, Old Habits	18
The Landscape of Rest	22
Rest: The Weapon against Sin	26
What Is the Gospel?	29
About the authors	33
Also by Theocast	39

INTRODUCTION

JON MOFFITT

Many Christians evaluate their lives and ask the same questions: Am I doing enough? Have I shown enough discipline, enough dedication, or enough effort? Would praying and reading my Bible more help me overcome . . . remove . . . have . . . You may feel that you put so much effort into improving your Christian life with no apparent fruit. Sins you thought would have been easier to overcome are still plaguing your daily life.

The common solution to doubting, fearing, or backsliding is to try harder, be more disciplined, or find an accountability partner. After a while, many begin to simply fake their security and happiness. We pretend that we feel excited about our walk with God, that we never wonder if He is pleased with us. Those around us who are faithfully reading their Bibles, journaling, and having morning prayer time seem to have their lives all put together. You never hear them complain or struggle with life. If it works for them, why doesn't it work for me? Most feel they aren't doing enough compared to those who have radically given so much to the church, to the poor, or to the mission field. Sermons are not refreshing but serve as reminders of how far you have fallen, or how far behind you are from everyone else. Week after week, the list becomes more and more impossible to complete. You probably even doubt your salvation at times. Thoughts creep into your head, "How could I truly be a Christian if I still struggle with the same sin year after year? I don't have the same excitement as other Christians. I don't desire to read my Bible an hour each day. Am I the real thing?"

You are not alone, and you are not crazy! Many Christians today live on this sort of performance-based treadmill, running fast and getting nowhere. Trying harder and doing more haven't produced assurance or victory over sin. You're exhausted. You feel empty and fake inside. You feel guilty for merely wanting to just coast, to give in, to stop trying.

The foundation of Christianity is faith. And the foundation of the Christian faith, we will argue in this primer, is rest. It is obvious that this important reality of the Christian experience appears at the bottom of the list in messages emphasized today (if it makes it at all). "Rest comes when Christ returns," the logic goes. Celebration of a victory should be at the *end* of the race, not before. The weary pilgrim is exhorted to sing, "Onward, Christian soldiers, marching as to war!" And what is it that we are fighting for? Assurance, acceptability, and blessings from God. These are granted once we faithfully perform our Christian duties. But what level of faithfulness does the Bible require? How many mistakes until your assurance, acceptability, or blessings are called into question? We are warned that a healthy relationship with God is like a healthy lifestyle. You slow down on working out and eating healthy, and your body will respond negatively.

Most evangelical Christians would wholeheartedly affirm that we are saved by grace alone through faith alone. But, after salvation, there is much work to be done to prove that you are truly saved and to receive blessings from God. This comes to us in many different forms—sermons with five key elements to overcoming this problem, books with three insights to conquering the setbacks of that sin, and conferences promoting four strategies to a better *whatever* . . . you get the point. The priority of the modern Christian message is concentrated on the successful Christian life. The key to success? Your faithfulness to some new code. And when that code doesn't work, there are other options to explore that promise a new outcome. Many are striving for rest and yet never finding it. What stands in their way is their own performance. It just never feels as if it is enough. When will God finally look upon me and say, "Well done!"? It is the constant Christian hamster wheel. The harder we try, the more exhausted we feel, and there is still no progress.

For the last few years, Theocast has been attempting to point out that this emphasis on our own faithfulness is a movement identified as *pietism*. We are endeavoring to point this out in contrast to *confessionalism*. These two descriptors are in constant rotation within the ministry of Theocast. Over the years, as we have sought to clarify and define our perspective, we have found these terms helpful. The meaning of these expressions (as we have employed them) are not mysterious to those who follow our ministry. Whether they've used the expression or not, most people know exactly what we mean when we say "pietism." For most, it's as if we are finally putting words to what they've been thinking for a long time.

Our objective is not to present an exhaustive explanation of these two terms, but to offer a simple classification to start your journey toward resting in Christ. We pray that you will be able to identify where pietism has entered your Christian faith and to turn toward trusting in the power of the gospel.

WHAT IS PIETISM?

JUSTIN PERDUE

We should start with the difference between *piety* and *pietism*. To put it simply, piety is godliness. Piety is good. God works in us by His Holy Spirit. He sanctifies us. In that sense, piety incorporates transformation. To be crystal clear, we are all for piety. In pushing back against pietism, we are not pushing back against biblical piety. Our hope is that the difference will become clear as you keep reading and listening.

Pietism could be defined as hyper-piety. In pietism, there is an overemphasis on the life of the Christian and what the Christian should be doing. The experience of the Christian and the interior of the Christian's life are paramount. Pietism tends to place these realities above all others and makes them the focus. And so, in a pietistic context, almost all instruction is aimed at how the Christian should live.

Pietism begins with the question: What must we do? This is the baseline consideration. As a result, duty (what we do) comes before identity (who we are) in a pietistic world.

Even worse, in this schema, our identity is seemingly derived from what we do—or don't do—and assurance is tethered to how well we're performing our duty. If we aren't performing well, we should be worried.

Within pietism, there is also an obsession with ongoing improvement. We must always be getting better. We need to have ever-increasing amounts of "victory" over sin. We need to be growing in personal holiness—daily. Our feelings about Jesus need to keep getting better and better. Our sense of satisfaction in God needs to be continually on the up and up. There is a tendency to try to measure progress in these areas like we would a child's height against the wall. And the message is that if there isn't sufficient progress in these things (who defines that standard, by the way?), we should be concerned about our standing before God.

To be clear, the concern with pietism is not that Christ and His work are missing altogether. That would be an unfair characterization. In almost all pietistic contexts, Christ and His work are preached. The concern with pietism is that Christ and His work are in the background, rather than the foreground. Pietism is an ideology that is preoccupied with piety and, therefore, puts the Christian life in the foreground, with Christ as the backdrop. In essence, pietism focuses on the Christian rather than on Christ.

It should be noted that pietism is essentially a response to an opposite error: hyper-orthodoxy (or, as it is sometimes called, "dead orthodoxy"). With hyper-orthodoxy, there is an emphasis on clarity of doctrine to the neglect of how we are to live. This error should be pushed back against;

however, when a collective overreaction occurs against hyper-orthodoxy the result is pietism.

There is one more thing, and this is critical for our understanding: *Evangelicalism is a pietistic movement.* Pietism and revivalism have shaped the evangelical church in America. And so, pietism is ubiquitous in the American church. It's like white noise. It's the water we swim in and the air we breathe. For most of us who have come of age in the evangelical church, pietism is our default setting.

WHAT IS CONFESSIONALISM?

JUSTIN PERDUE

Confessionalism has a completely different emphasis than pietism. Here, the emphasis is on objective (outside of us) and declarative (done/finished) realities that are to be confessed, believed, and trusted. These objective, declarative realities center on Christ and His work.

We do look back to the confessions of faith that were produced during the era of the Reformation. These confessions arose, as confessions typically do, because theological clarity was required. The Reformation was a response to the rampant moralism and works-based system of the medieval church. Therefore, the confessions that were produced out of it push back against moralism.

Confessionalism emphasizes Jesus and what He has accomplished on our behalf. The emphasis is on what has been *done*. The concern, in a confessional context, is that we take hold of—and rest in—our standing before God *in Christ*, regardless of how we might be feeling or performing at any given moment. If the Christian is at the center in pietism, Christ is at the center in confessionalism. Jesus and His work are in the foreground; the Christian life is in the background and is only rightly understood in light of Jesus and His accomplishments.

Confessionalism begins with the question: Who are we? This is the baseline consideration. As a result, identity precedes duty in a confessional world. What we do is derived from who we are, not the other way around. Here, assurance is dependent on Christ and His work—and our identity in Him. We are pointed to Jesus, not our efforts or performance. To be clear, there is plenty of instruction on how we live within confessionalism. There are plenty of practical considerations. The key is that the finished work of Christ is heralded and kept at the center of the believer's focus. Another way to put it is that Christ's work precedes that of the Christian. In a confessional context, we speak substantially to piety (the Reformed confessions do). However, the motivation for piety never moves outside of what Jesus has already accomplished for us, and the realization of piety is never outside of the Holy Spirit's work in us.

HOW DO I KNOW IF I'M IN A PIETISTIC CONTEXT?

JUSTIN PERDUE

You might be wondering, "How do I know if I'm in a pietistic context?" This is by no means an exhaustive list. Our aim is to help you practically understand the differences in perspectives.

1. The place of the gospel. In a *pietistic* context, the gospel is usually viewed as the entry point to the Christian life. Our conversion, which was the point we came to believe the gospel, happened "back there," and now we are moving on to matters of the Christian life, which becomes the focus.

In a *confessional* context, the gospel is the ground of our confidence, always. We live in it and under it, always. We need the gospel just as much today as the day we were converted.

2. The gospel in the corporate service. In a *pietistic* context, the gospel is often a kind of a footnote in the corporate gathering. It's mentioned. The plan of salvation is laid out—perhaps during the sermon or at the end of the service. Or, maybe, the gospel is assumed. It's alluded to. In all of this though, the focus is something else. Another huge point is that in pietism, the gospel is primarily applied to the non-believer. After all, as pietistic thinking goes, the non-believer is the one who really needs the gospel.

In a *confessional* context, the gospel permeates every aspect of the service—from the preaching to the prayers, to the songs, to the Lord's Supper. (Even the welcome might include comments on the gospel and our desperate need for Jesus and His work in our place!) In a confessional context, too, the gospel is primarily applied to the redeemed. Of course, any non-believers in attendance would hear this and might even be addressed directly, but the understanding is that the redeemed need Christ held out to them every time they gather.

3. Law and gospel. In *pietism*, law and gospel are often mixed. In some cases, the law is preached as gospel (obey well enough in order to be saved), and the gospel is preached as law (e.g., the "demands of the gospel").

In *confessionalism*, a proper distinction is maintained between the law and the gospel. The law is good; however, we can't keep and fulfill all it requires. The law condemns us and drives us to Jesus, who kept it perfectly in our place. Upon conversion, the law is the guide for the believer's life. The gospel is the message of Jesus, who alone accomplished redemption. He is to be trusted. Jesus did the gospel; believers don't "do the gospel."

4. Tone. To be clear, when we say "tone," we are referring to the tone and tenor of the preaching, teaching, leadership, and general interactions amongst the saints in the church. In a *pietistic* environment, the tone is often exacting—or even threatening. Much of the teaching and a lot of the interactions have an edge to them. The focus tends to be on the demands placed on the believer—and how the believer has failed and needs to do better.

In a *confessional* environment, the tone is usually compassionate. There is an understanding that the struggle against sin and corruption is hard. Sin is taken seriously, and at the same time, the church feels safe. The focus is most often on Jesus—and how He has paid for the sin of the believer and provided righteousness for him or her. Teaching on how we are to live takes place under that banner. Confessionalism focuses on Christ and Him crucified *for us*.

5. Assurance. In *pietism*, there is often an erosion of assurance in order to motivate people toward personal holiness or participation in church life. Assurance is often presented as the pursuit of the Christian life—it's the thing we're chasing after.

In *confessionalism*, there is a conscious effort to bolster assurance by pointing the believer to Christ and His righteousness that is his or hers by faith. Assurance is presented as the essence of the Christian life, rather than the pursuit of the Christian life. Assurance is the baseline.

6. Motivation. In a *pietistic* context, the motivation—to press on in the Christian life, to pursue holiness, and to participate in church—is often doubt, fear, and worry. The thinking is that the believer needs to be unsettled in order to be motivated. And, what's more, if we keep telling people they're righteous in Christ and have nothing to fear, they'll just go on sinning and be content with moral laxity and spiritual laziness.

In a *confessional* context, the motivation for the Christian life is usually assurance and security in Jesus. We really are safe in Christ. And we are driven by love, joy, gratitude, and delight to pursue holiness, obedience, and love. Our union with Christ by faith and the presence of the Holy Spirit in us propel us forward.

7. Means of spiritual growth. In *pietism*, the emphasis is almost exclusively on personal spiritual disciplines as the means of spiritual growth. Ordinary means of grace, which are predominantly corporate realities, are not considered much, if at all. And when they are, they're seen as supplements to the really important stuff—which happens in private.

In *confessionalism*, the emphasis is on the ordinary means of grace. These means include the Word of God, sacrament (baptism and the Lord's Supper), church (people of God), prayer, and song. These means show up in a unique way when the church is gathered. Certainly, personal time in the Word and prayer, amongst other things, are wonderful, but these things are viewed as a supplement to the believer's participation in the corporate life of the body.

8. Focus (where the believer is pointed). In a *pietistic* environment, believers are usually pointed inside themselves—to the transformation of their lives. The Christian is at the center of the focus.

In a *confessional* environment, believers are usually pointed outside themselves—to the righteousness of Christ. Jesus is at the center of the focus.

9. The "front burner" concern. In a *pietistic* context, the front burner concern—the thing that is always in the crosshairs—is nominalism. (To be nominal is to be Christian in name only, that is, a false professor.) The assumption is that the local church is full of nominal people who need to be smoked out. This assumption is clear in preaching and teaching, as well as in how the Bible is understood and applied.

In a *confessional* context, the front burner concern is moralism. The assumption here is that people tend to weave their works into the fabric of their salvation—that is, we are always prone to think our standing before God is at stake in the way we perform, and we tend to think we do good works for merit. From the confessional perspective, the way to combat nominalism is not more law; it is gospel clarity and union with Christ.

10. Understanding of the sacraments. In *pietism*, the sacraments of baptism and the Lord's Supper are primarily seen as acts of our personal devotion. This is why, for example, the Lord's Supper is a time of anxiety and panic for many. The emphasis of the Supper moment is the faithfulness of the believer (or lack thereof).

In *confessionalism*, the sacraments are seen as signs of God's faithfulness to us, not our faithfulness to Him. We look back to our baptism and know that we have been cleansed and united to Christ; we will be finally saved in Him. We come to the Table together to remember what Jesus accomplished for us, to proclaim His death until He comes, and to assure one another that we are good with God in Christ.

11. How theology is done. In a *pietistic* context, theology is largely an individual exercise. Believers tend to identify with a particular person and his teaching—or maybe a particular church—rather than a historic confession, a historic tradition, or the history of interpretation.

In a *confessional* context, theology is largely a corporate exercise. Believers tend to identify with a historic confession, a historic tradition, the *regulae fide* (rule of faith), and the history of interpretation. Only the Scriptures are our infallible guide. And at the same time, there is an understanding that the same Holy Spirit has been working in the church for 2,000 years. This has produced a common confession and heritage of orthodoxy.

HOW CONFESSIONALISM LEADS TO REST

JUSTIN PERDUE

Here at Theocast, we believe the confessional perspective to be the most accurate and sound understanding of Scripture. We are also convinced that this conversation about confessionalism and pietism matters for local churches and believers who comprise them. This is far from an academic theological debate. These things matter for our lives. Every day. This is because confessionalism is the only perspective that offers the believer rest.

1. A confessional perspective offers the believer real peace and assurance. Many of us have lived in a church context where we have been repeatedly pointed inward. Diagnostic questions abound, and they demand quantified answers. How well are we obeying God's commands? How well are we fighting temptation? How well are we mortifying sin? What about our affections? Are they where they should be?

For many of us, our assurance and peace with God have been tethered to how well we are performing—or feeling—on any given day. We've been taught (explicitly or implicitly) we can only be assured to the extent that we are sanctified. Essentially, we have been pointed to the transformation of our lives as the ground of our confidence. Friend, that is sinking sand. How in the world can we have any assurance or peace before God if our salvation depends upon our faithfulness to any degree?

For anyone in a context where the focus is on what Christians need to be doing and on how well they are doing it, the Christian life can feel like a perpetual uphill climb. It's exhausting. There is no rest for the weary pilgrim. Our consciences already haunt us. And then it's just piled on. There is always more to do. Things can always be done better.

Confessionalism points us outside of ourselves to the finished work of Christ (John 19:30; Hebrews 10:12). Christ has provided us with righteousness by fulfilling God's law in our place (Romans 5:19; Galatians 4:4-5). He has atoned for our sin. He has satisfied the wrath of God for us (Romans 3:24-25; 1 John 2:2). He is our resurrection and our life (John 11:25-26; Romans 6:4-5). The emphasis, in a confessional world, is that Jesus has accomplished everything necessary for our salvation (Hebrews 10:11-14). The work is finished. There is nothing left to do. Our salvation is certain—because of Jesus. And so, we have assurance (John 6:37-40, 10:28; Hebrews 7:25). Our standing before God is secure, and we are safe. Jesus has seen to that (Romans 5:1, 8:1).

In Christ, we are given grace because we're sinners. We are given peace because we have troubled consciences. We feel like God's enemies, but He has told us we are His children

(Romans 8:15). We really are good with God, and He is good with us. On the solid rock of Jesus and His merit, we find a sure place to rest.

2. A confessional perspective offers the believer hope in the midst of the struggle. This is related to what we just considered. If our hope is tethered to our faithfulness and performance, what happens to our hope when we are really struggling in our fight against sin and temptation? Where is our hope in the midst of trial when our faith is weak and our love is cold? There isn't any.

In a confessional context, there is hope in the midst of difficulty and struggle. This is because our hope and confidence are in Jesus alone—on our best day or our worst day. In the midst of the deepest wrestlings and darkest doubts, the objective, declarative realities of Christ and the gospel change the game. How I'm doing or feeling doesn't change what Christ has done. Not at all. Christ—and His finished work—is the resting place when our zeal and our joy are nowhere to be found. It is Christ's love for us, not our love for Him, that will carry the day. The struggle is real. And in the struggle, we have hope. It is this hope that allows us to rest. It leads us to rest in what Christ has done and not labor to prove our right standing before God.

3. A confessional perspective helps us see sanctification as a certainty—and a delight. Have you been in a church context where believers are scolded toward obedience? Sadly, it's common. The tone is often exacting or even threatening. The idea here is that people need to have skin in the game in order to take holiness seriously. Merit, fear,

and dread are often seen as the motivators for sanctification. The message tends to come across, "You better get it together . . . or else." Underneath all of this is one of two assumptions: either people in the church are nominal (and, therefore, don't really care about growth in holiness), or sanctification is uncertain (and, therefore, we've got to get on people to make sure it happens). In this context, obedience often comes across like a trip to the DMV.

In a confessional world though, our sanctification is as certain as our present justification and future glorification. Let that sink in for a minute. Fact: God will sanctify all those He has justified through Christ. "For those whom he foreknew he also predestined to be conformed to the image of his Son, in order that he might be the firstborn among many brothers" (Romans 8:29).

At this point, it might be beneficial to respond to a common objection. People get all kinds of concerned when we preach that Jesus has accomplished everything necessary for salvation and that there is nothing left to do. The objection goes like this, "If you keep telling people that Christ is their righteousness, that the work of redemption is over, and that all there is to do now is trust and rest in Jesus, you will produce apathetic people who don't give a rip about obedience."

The problem with that objection is that it doesn't square with the Bible. That objection demonstrates a misunderstanding of the gospel and the new birth. Two things need to be said here. First, upon trusting Christ, we have a new identity. Second, the Holy Spirit, who dwells in us, will sanctify us. Think about Paul's response to the objection that the gospel means we can sin all the more (Romans 6:1ff). He doesn't refute that charge by upping the ante with more law. He responds with the believer's union with Christ by faith. We are now *in Christ*. We have been delivered from the dominion of sin. In that sense, we obey because we can! The Holy Spirit has sealed us for the day of salvation (Ephesians 1:13-14). He will complete the good work He has started in us (Philippians 1:6). He will conform us to the image of Jesus (Romans 8:29).

You see, biblically, safety and assurance are motivators for obedience. So is love. And joy. And gratitude toward God. From a confessional perspective, our obedience is driven by delight, not dread.

4. A confessional perspective makes the church a safe place. For many, the church is the place where they feel the least safe. It's the last place in the world they would ever want to open up about deep struggles and ugly sins. This is true in large part because the posture in many churches is, "You should be better by now." In such an environment, the people who do open up about their failings are often run over—or run out of town on a rail. Many can probably recall a situation of getting up the nerve to share something difficult in the church and going away thinking, "Well, I'll never do that again."

In a confessional context, there is the understanding that the Christian is at the same time justified and sinner. It's expected that Christians will struggle with sin and corruption—even Christians with good theology. Everyone understands that sin is normal, and it's not okay. We're not condoning ridiculous behavior. We're not giving sin a pass. We're simply acknowledging the internal war is real (Romans 7:15ff; Galatians 5:17). When people fail and fall, we're not surprised. When believers are ensnared in sin, others come alongside them with compassion (Galatians 6:1). The instinctive response isn't, "You should be better by now." Instead, the response is, "I'm sorry. This is really hard. Remember, Christ is your righteousness. I'm here. Let's talk." We lean in toward the person who has confessed sin—rather than pushing away in repulsion. Instead of being shamed and run over, the struggling Christian is met with compassion and love. This is because of a biblical understanding of sin and the work of Christ. We inherited the corruption of Adam (Romans 5:12-19). We are in a state of sin. There is a misery associated with being a fallen human being (Genesis 3:16-19). And Jesus has justified us. We don't justify ourselves. He is our righteousness. With all of this in view, the church becomes a haven for the weary pilgrim—a place of rest and safety.

Remember the words of our Lord: "Come to me, all who labor and are heavy laden, and I will give you rest. Take my yoke upon you, and learn from me, for I am gentle and lowly in heart, and you will find rest for your souls. For my yoke is easy, and my burden is light" (Matthew 11:28-30). Amen.

NEW CREATURES, OLD HABITS

JIMMY BUEHLER, JUSTIN PERDUE, & JON MOFFITT

What is the Christian's relationship with sin? This question is foundational if we want to make sense of what the Christian's life is supposed to look like. Understanding our current state and situation will help us understand how we should see ourselves before God and others. Sure, before we were saved, we were "dead in our trespasses and sins" and "alienated and hostile in mind, doing evil deeds" (Ephesians 2:1; Colossians 1:21). At that point, we could do nothing but sin. And in our future, glorified state, we will never sin again. We will do nothing but good. But what about right now?

Right off the bat, we need to acknowledge that we're different than we were before we were converted. Paul is clear that we are a new creation and that sin no longer has dominion over us (2 Corinthians 5:17; Romans 6:14). As soon as we were connected to Christ by faith, sin ceased to be our master. It no longer holds its enslaving power over us.

We must also admit that, in this life, all of us are deeply troubled with sin! Paul says, concerning his post-conversion self, "I know that nothing good dwells in me, that is, in my flesh. For I have the desire to do what is right, but not the ability to carry it out" (Romans 7:18). Our own experience tells us that the apostle Paul is exactly right. The internal war is real. Our flesh wages war against our spirit to keep us from doing what we want to do (Galatians 5:17). To say, as some do, that the Christian can attain sinlessness in this life is a denial of the biblical witness—as well as a tremendous underestimation of what God's law actually requires.

A helpful category for spelling this out is Luther's phrase that we are *simul justus et peccator*, which means "simultaneously saint and sinner." We are justified sinners. Now, this seems to be a contradiction in terms. From our perspective, we see ourselves to be sinners based on our actions and thoughts. But at the same time, in the eyes of God, we *are* righteous because we are clothed in the perfection of Jesus—not our own righteousness but "the righteousness from God that depends on faith" (Philippians 3:9).

It is essential to understand the distinction between these two perspectives in order to rest in your salvation! When you struggle with sin, it does not affect your standing before God. Your verdict of "not guilty" still stands unchanged. When you are faithless, He remains faithful (2 Timothy 2:13).

Now, to be sure, God has given us the Spirit, who wages war against our sinful nature, to create good works in us.

This is actually what creates the internal struggle within the believer. On the one hand, our old man lies within us, seeking to rebel against the law of God revealed through His Word and written on our hearts. On the other hand, the Spirit that raised Jesus from the dead now dwells in us, resurrecting our dead selves to new life and causing us to desire to love God and neighbor (Romans 8:10-11). This is the daily battle of the Christian life. In possibly the most relatable verses of the Bible, Paul says, "For I do not do the good I want, but the evil I do not want is what I keep on doing" (Romans 7:19). The Christian lives in this tension.

Of course, we hate the idea that the Christian life is a long struggle against sin, but there is actually something rather comforting in the truth of this tension. It lies in the fact that the struggle is *normal* for the Christian who hasn't yet passed into glory. Often when we struggle with sin, we start to doubt our own salvation. We start to wonder if it's really possible for a Christian to still be sinning after [insert number] years of knowing Christ. The idea of being simultaneously saint and sinner tells us that our situation is normal—there is no need to freak out and worry about the state of our salvation.

And this is the truth that helps us continue to battle our sin, because it is this truth that keeps us confessing our sins to God without fear! We don't have to worry about our standing before God. We know the Father has forgiven us in Christ, and we can confess our sins, knowing He is faithful and just to forgive us our sins. We can keep going back to God with our sins, because we know that in His eyes we are still righteous. We can be confident that He will not kick us out of the family.

It is the Spirit that reveals to us our sin, causing us to admit that we have failed to keep God's law. The Spirit then pushes us to trust in Christ more, since He is our only hope of peace. And the Spirit continues to work at our desires at the heart level, causing us to trust more and more in Christ and less in ourselves. In this way, the Spirit is resurrecting us now, giving us a taste of the future resurrection. However, in this life, it really is only a taste.

Simul justus et peccator is not a slogan to cause us to lower our standards—the standard of God's law doesn't change. It does, however, help us run to our Savior when we find ourselves sinning. It reminds us of the irrevocable gifts the Father has lavished on us because of the work of Christ. We will continue to sin, but He will continue to smile upon us. Truly nothing, not even ourselves, can separate us from the love of God in Christ Jesus our Lord.

THE LANDSCAPE OF REST

JON MOFFITT

When you move to *living* status forward (from *should* to *am*), the landscape will appear very different. Our status is locked up in the finished work of Christ. His perfect obedience was placed into our account, and God only sees us as righteous. There is nothing that can separate us from that act of love granted to us by grace. When you feel this reality of a new status, your heart will never skip a beat, wondering if you made the wrong choice. Worry fades away into the blood of Christ, for He covered all your sins. As children, we are handed a new wardrobe. We have a uniform with "Justified" embroidered on the front to remind us of our status. This is permanently ours. Nothing we ever do or fail to do can cause the Father to take our family crest away. Not only does He provide a new wardrobe, but He also provides new food. The Father constantly feeds us by His simple means of grace. Bread and wine are given to celebrate time and time again the joy of our salvation. Christ comes and communes with us, assuring us we belong to Him. Our faith is infused with greater strength in His mediation. At the Table of God, we are never encouraged to look to our performance, instead we remember what Christ has done on our behalf. The Father then graciously takes His perfect inspired Word and has it spoken over us week after week. We hear the constant refrain, "I am faithful to My promises. I have promised to make you Mine, and you are Mine." From Genesis forward, sinners are redeemed not by their own faithfulness but always by the faithfulness of a gracious God.

Knowing that His children remain in their broken sinful bodies, the Father places us into local families. These families (churches) are for the care and protection of His precious children. While they await the return of the Son, they have been given a mission. This mission is the primary focus of their life now that they are His children. Their mission is twofold: build up the faith of the other family members among them and spread the gospel message to the world (Ephesians 4:11-16). Church is never where we prove ourselves to the Father. The Father never questions who belongs to Him. Therefore, church is where the following happens:

· We are reminded of whom we belong to. We often fall into fear and doubt because of the sin that remains.

· We find our reminder to rest not in ourselves but in Christ.

· We help those who are trapped and weary and lead them back to the refreshment of Christ.

· We are refreshed and drink His Word week after week.

Feasting on Christ creates joyful anticipation within weary pilgrims. They know they will receive living waters and eternal bread that will replenish their souls. To love the family comes to us as a command, but we obey it out of joy. Why? Because of the great love we have received. We love because we have experienced the love of God first (1 John 4:19)

The Father's instructions to His family are not burdensome. We see His holiness, His glory, His beauty in these commands and worship in obedience. As a child learning to color within the lines, we happily perform our Christian duties, knowing all the while we are imperfect. We will never be able to perfectly love the Father or our family members, but we joyfully continue to color, knowing the Father is pleased with our efforts. Our good works are also covered in our status as righteous. It is a new experience to imperfectly obey and know the Father will accept it. The primary message we hear sung to us is not what we must do for the Father but what the Father has done for us. It keeps us motivated to always look to the Son. We are good because the Son has provided our needed status. It is here we seek to bring others into this joy of rest.

Within a confessional context, the church is not where we go to self improve but where we live with our family to grow in grace together. Pietism is heavily individualized, focusing on our own spiritual progress. In this new landscape of confessionalism, we look not to ourselves but to the body to evaluate our spiritual health. Paul provides specific details of how the church is to function as a unit, as a body with many members (1 Corinthians 12-27). We are not all disconnected units seeking self-improvement, but one body functioning to grow together. Paul concludes, "From whom the whole body, joined and held together by every joint with which it is equipped, when each part is working properly, makes the body grow so that it builds itself up in love" (Ephesians 4:16).

When transitioning from pietism to rest, the church becomes our home away from home. Within the church, we find the constant refrain of the gospel pointing us to our final rest in glory with the Father. When the world attempts to rob us of this rest, to lead us back into pietism or sin, our brothers and sisters are there to confront us, encourage us, and carry us when we cannot walk on our own. Our consideration moves from self-improvement to love and care for our family. We ask not how am I doing, but how are we doing. "The Christian life was never intended to be lived alone" is a constant phrase we remind those who follow Theocast. Podcasts, books, and online sermons are great, but they can never replace the God-given treasure of His church.

When the gospel is the center of the church's life, it removes many of the struggles it faces with gossip, bitterness, selfishness, and laziness. To be clear, no church will be free from the presence of sin. The very nature of the church is to help limping Christians deal with the frailty of their lives. But together we can find rest knowing we are all equally in need of God's mercy and grace.

REST: THE WEAPON AGAINST SIN

JON MOFFITT

When we sin, we are attempting to find satisfaction in something other than God. Sin tempts us to add to what God has provided for us in Christ. Pride is forgetting we are all equally in need of grace. Fear is forgetting God is sovereign. Lust is forgetting the promises of God. Anger is forgetting the mercy of God. Laziness is forgetting the provisions of God. I'm sure you can see and make many other connections. When our hearts are tempted by sin, we will first move away from resting in the goodness of God. Fighting sin is fighting to rest. This is why the doctrine of justification (saved by grace through faith alone) is so important to our daily lives. Securing our eternal hope allows us to expose the lies of this temporal world. Our justification secures our future home. That home will be eternally satisfying, for it will be in the presence of the Son. In anticipation, we rest in this promise. Hebrews 12 tells us to "lay aside every weight, and sin which clings so closely, and let us run with endurance the race that is set before us, looking to Jesus, the founder and perfecter of our faith."

The fight against sin begins by looking to Christ, by resting in what He has done for us. We set aside anything that would prevent us from pursuing Christ. As stated above, the old man still barks at us. We will never outlive the temptation of sin in this life.

Luther observed, "A godly man feels sin more than grace, wrath more than favor, judgment more than redemption." We often strive to remove these feelings. The sin that remains will always keep us in our humble position. When we look at Christ, we can clearly see the need to find our satisfaction in Him and nothing else. The London Baptist Confession helpfully reminds us,

> The most wise, righteous, and gracious God doth oftentimes leave for a season his own children to manifold temptations and the corruptions of their own hearts, to chastise them for their former sins, or to discover unto them the hidden strength of corruption and deceitfulness of their hearts, that they may be humbled; and to raise them to a more close and constant dependence for their support upon himself; and to make them more watchful against all future occasions of sin, and for other just and holy ends. (LBCF ch.5.5)

Our sin should cause us to run to find our rest in Christ once again. Sin is the reminder that nothing in this world can satisfy, sustain, or bring lasting joy outside of Christ. This is why the writer of Hebrews encouraged the church to, "exhort one another every day, as long as it is called 'today,' that none of you may be hardened by the deceitfulness of sin" (Hebrews 3:13). The gospel is not the starting point of our journey, it is what carries us in our journey. The gospel is what brings light to our path. It is what guides us away from self-justification. It is what keeps us humble and in need of more grace. The gospel is the greatest weapon against the temptations of sin.

WHAT IS THE GOSPEL?

JIMMY BUEHLER

As we think about the Christian faith and life, the central message is the gospel. It's a loaded word. But what is it? We have already mentioned it throughout this primer, but we do not want to assume its meaning. In other words, because the word "gospel" is thrown to and fro within the broader Christian church, the one thing we *can* assume is that its meaning has been muddled or confused. Therefore, allow us to present a simple definition of what we mean by gospel:

The gospel is a declarative announcement that God has defeated the powers of sin and death, and that He has saved sinners through the perfect life, death, and resurrection of His Son, Jesus Christ, and that by grace alone, through faith alone, the perfect righteousness of Christ is imputed, or credited, to the accounts of sinners.

In the message and content of the gospel, we hear words like "sin" and "death" frequently (Romans 3:9, 23). This is what we understand as the "bad news." That is, in and of yourself, you are dead in sin (Ephesians 2:1-3). When we look at God's perfect standard of holiness, His law, it confronts us like a mirror. This is where some misunderstanding has crept into our view of the gospel. That is, you may respond, "I have never murdered someone" (God's sixth commandment) or, "I have never committed adultery" (God's seventh commandment). But Jesus does not allow us to get off that easy. Rather, in the Sermon on the Mount, Jesus claims that those who have been angry with their brother or lusted after another person indeed *have* committed murder and adultery (Matthew 5:21-30). In our legalistic hearts and minds, we can look at God's commandments as a ladder to climb rather than a mirror to confront. We can view God's commandments as the means by which we achieve holiness, righteousness, and relationship with God. Take Jesus' summation of the entire law in Luke 10:27: "You shall love the Lord your God with all your heart and with all your soul and with all your strength and with all your mind, and your neighbor as yourself."

Now, realistically assess yourself. Think of your daily routines. Think of your daily interactions. Would you say that *every* word you say, *every* thought you think *perfectly* displays that you love God with all your heart, soul, mind, and strength *and* that you love your neighbor as yourself? We are not talking "I am trying," we are talking perfection (Galatians 3:10). Disobedience to these commandments in the slightest is sin, and its punishment from a just God is death. To extend this even further, this "sin" that you are guilty of is more than a mere collection of misdeeds on your part, it is a power in and over you and a state in which you live. This bad news is not "bad, but not awful," it is "bad, *and* condemning." So what hope is there that we, sinners by birth and sinners by choice, can stand before a holy and righteous God?

The word *gospel* literally means "good news." In its original setting, the Greek word for gospel (*euangelion*) was understood as an announcement of victory. So as we think about victory in terms of the gospel, what does that mean? In light of the bad news, that we are dead in sin and deserve death, the gospel tells us that the powers of sin and death have been defeated. The Scriptures are laden with the good news that God, through Christ, has initiated toward sinners in grace, love, and mercy (Ephesians 2:4-8; Titus 3:5; John 3:16). The perfect law that condemns us? Jesus perfectly fulfilled it. The powers of sin and death that held us captive? Jesus' death and resurrection defeated them. This is what theologians have coined as the "passive and active obedience of Christ." That is, in His active obedience, Jesus perfectly fulfilled God's holy law; and in His passive obedience, Jesus bore the curse of sin at the cross in His death (Romans 10:4; Colossians 2:14; Galatians 3:23-25).

Here is where the gospel becomes good news: in the death of Christ we sinners can be forgiven of sin. And because of the perfect life of Christ, we are credited (imputed) the perfect righteousness of Christ by faith (2 Corinthians 5:21: Romans 1:17; Romans 10:4). When we understand the gospel this way, we see it not as something "we do" but rather as something "God *has done* in Christ." As Christians, we do not "live the gospel" or "do the gospel"—rather, we *believe* the gospel. Everything contained in the gospel is done *for* you. The active agent in the gospel is God, who has accomplished your salvation without any of your help. This gospel exists outside of you.

Dear weary pilgrim, rest in the gracious gospel of Christ! Know that you, dead in sin and unable to keep any of God's law, have been saved by the perfect person and work of Jesus Christ. Your forgiveness is not contingent upon the quality of your holiness, the sincerity of your repentance, or the strength of your faith. Your forgiveness, assurance, and rest are freely given to you in the promises of Jesus Christ and made effective because of the *object* of your faith. *This* is the gospel. This is what we declare to you—that there is good news! The God that you have offended with your sin has forgiven you. The righteousness He requires of you, He has also provided for you in the meritorious work of His Son, Jesus Christ. Think of it like this: what God demanded of you in His law, He has provided for you in His gospel. Believe and rest in that by grace alone through faith alone, on account of Christ alone, you are forgiven!

ABOUT THE AUTHORS

Our primary focus at Theocast is to encourage weary pilgrims to rest in Christ. We facilitate simple conversations about the Christian life from a reformed perspective through our weekly podcasts, primers, books, blogs, and educational material.

Jon Moffitt - Senior pastor of Community Bible Church in Spring Hill, TN

Jon was born and raised in the sunny desert of Southern California. Jon is married to Judith, and they have four children: Charis, Titus, Jane, and Knox.

Jon's father was a pastor for 25 years in California before moving to Utah where the Lord took him home in 2002. After graduating from college in CA, Jon spent several years working in a small church as a youth pastor in Utah. It was while ministering there that he began to feel the need for more theological training and moved back to CA to attend seminary.

While in seminary, he became involved in a local church as the college and young adults pastor until graduating in December of 2011. Thirty days later, with his wife and three kids, Jon moved to Nashville, TN to become the

Young Adult Pastor at Community Bible Church. In 2017 Jon was sent out to plan Community Bible Church in Spring Hill, TN. Jon is one of the founding members and director of Theocast Ministries.

Social Media: Twitter: @jonmoffitt

Community Bible Church:

Website: communitysouth.org

Twitter & Instagram: @cbcsouth

Sermons: *Sermon Audio* on your favorite podcast app or at communitysouth.org/listen

Jimmy Buehler - Senior pastor of Christ Community Church in Willmar, MN

Jimmy was born and raised in Toledo, OH and attended a small church of loving believers. In bible college, Jimmy was blessed to sit under God-centered teaching and preaching. It was during his time in a Calvinistic college ministry that the gospel became the focus and full-time ministry became a deep desire.

Jimmy has served in various ways in various churches since 2011. During this time, the ups and downs of ministry served to push him into deeper Reformed thinking and study. After a long battle with depression and crippling doubt, a friend of Jimmy sent him a podcast episode called "Leaving Pietism." That episode forever shifted his theological trajectory. This introduction into Reformed confessionalism has lead him to partner with Jon Moffitt in church planting efforts in his current town of Willmar, MN.

Jimmy is married to his wife, Kelsey, and together they have three children: Charlie, Owen, and Nora. The Buehlers currently reside in Willmar, MN and love the small, rural town which they serve. When they are not working with their photography business or with their church plant, the Buehlers like to eat smoked meats and enjoy evenings on their front porch. Jimmy also likes to enjoy his favorite sports team: Liverpool F.C. (Go Reds). Jimmy desires to help others see the rest found in Christ alone. Jimmy firmly believes that God used Reformed theology to save his life, and he is eager to point others to the glorious Jesus this historic theology portrays!

Social Media: Twitter: @buehlerjimmy

Christ Community Church:

Website: christcommunitymn.org

Twitter: @christccmn

Instagram: @christccmn

Facebook: @christccmn

Sermons: christcommunitymn.org

Justin Perdue - Senior pastor of Covenant Baptist Church in Asheville, NC

Justin was born in Newport News, VA but grew up in Asheville, NC. His formative years were spent in a Baptist church that was theologically liberal and culturally moralistic (yeah, the worst of every world). He grew up thinking Jesus was legit and the church was whack.

Justin played football at Furman University and majored in business administration. After college, he began a career in business with no thoughts of ever going into vocational ministry. In his early to mid-twenties, Justin was exposed to good teaching for the first time. His life began to change. He was given regular teaching and leadership opportunities in the church. Believers around him encouraged him to go into pastoral ministry, and, eventually, the Lord brought him to a place where that became his desire.

At the end of 2011, Justin moved to Washington, DC to do the pastoral internship at Capitol Hill Baptist Church and then went on staff there as a pastoral assistant. He and his family moved to Asheville in the summer of 2014 to begin the work of planting a church. Covenant Baptist Church was constituted in the fall of 2015. Justin still serves as the lead pastor of CBC.

Justin is married to Michelle. They met in early 2012 and were married at the end of that year. He knew he had found a good thing. Justin and Michelle have four kids: Josiah, Noelle, Titus, and Scottie. In addition to his family —and theology, of course—Justin enjoys the Asheville food and drink scene, music, and pretty much anything having to do with sports.

Social Media: Twitter: @justin_perdue

Covenant Baptist Church:

Website: covbap.org

Twitter: @cov_bap

Sermons: *Covenant Baptist Church Sermon Audio* on your favorite podcast app or at covbap.org/resources

Other content: functionaltheology.com

ALSO BY THEOCAST

A Pilgrim's Guide To Rest

Despite all the promises of scriptures, most Christians today are often left wondering if God is genuinely pleased with them. Their path feels like it leads from duty to acceptance. They strive every day to become the type of person that God would be pleased to save and call His own. Their trek is all uphill and filled with perpetual uncertainty. But this is not the flow of the Gospel - at least the one uncovered and rediscovered in the Reformation. The one defended by the Apostles. That Gospel always flows away from moralism. Life is lived from acceptance outward. We don't do what we do in order to earn God's love, but because we already have it. However, making that turn and heading back the opposite direction is no easy feat. Acceptance is a strange horizon when we've been conditioned to pursue assurance rather than rest in it. A Pilgrim's Guide to Rest is an explanation of what that turn looks like and the freedom it can yield to the weary pilgrim.

Made in the USA
Columbia, SC
05 November 2019